Crystal Healing

A guide to crystal healing, the human energy field, and how to improve your health with crystals!

Table of Contents

Introduction

Thank you for taking the time to read this book on crystal healing!

In the following chapters, you will learn about what crystal healing is, how it works, and what ailments it can assist in treating. You will discover exactly how to use crystals to improve your life, and will be provided with several methods for charging and energizing the crystals before use!

Also, you'll be provided with a comprehensive list of the different crystals commonly used, along with the associated benefits of each!

Crystal healing has been used for thousands of years, all around the world to help people overcome different ailments and improve their overall health and wellbeing. At the completion of this book you will have a good understanding of crystal healing, and be ready to try it out for yourself!

Once again, thanks for choosing this book, I hope you find it to be helpful!

Chapter 1: History of Crystals

Ancient Civilizations

Crystals have been around and in use the entire time humans have been in existence. Their wide usage began during the era of Ancient Egyptians, Greeks, and Chinese. Stones and crystals are even mentioned in the Bible several times.

Crystals started as healing tools, providing emotional and spiritual balance. As time passed by, crystals were promoted into being all-around gems. Ancient people used crystals as beauty tools, fashion pieces, and for parts of their rituals. The Japanese, for example, used crystals in their fortune-telling traditions.

The ancient Egyptians are popularly known for rubbing Rose Quartz crystals on their skin to maintain a glowing complexion. Cleopatra, one of the most powerful women in Ancient Egypt, is believed to have bathed with chunks of Rose Quartz to retain her youthfulness. Egyptian women also transformed Rose Quartz into a powder, and used it as a love potion ingredient, harnessing Rose Quartz' abilities to attract love. They also grounded Malachite into powdered form and used it akin to modern eye shadow.

Ancient Egyptians also used crystals in burial. They always put a crystal on a dead body's forehead; believing that a crystal had spiritual energy that would guide the dead's soul in the afterlife.

Ancient Sumerians used crystals as a tool for practicing their magical prowess.

Ancient Greeks were also advocates of using crystals for many different purposes. As a matter of fact, the names of many modern gems are derived from Greek terminologies.

The word "crystal" itself was derived from the Greek word "krustullos" which means ice. The Greeks believed that crystals were simply frozen water from the heavens. They used to rub Hematite or Iron Ore on their soldiers' bodies as a ritual of protection during war. Iron Ore is associated to Aries, the Greek God of war.

The Romans also used crystals in a similar manner. Their soldiers wore crystal talismans and amulets. They believed that the crystals would provide protection from their enemies and help them attract a good life.

Alongside the ancient Egyptians, the ancient Sumerians and Mesopotamians are also regarded as among the first civilizations to use crystals in the healing and energy department. They are believed to have adorned themselves with crystals such as Carnelian, Lapis Lazuli, and Turquoise in order to ward off negative energies and illnesses.

However, it was perhaps the Ancient Chinese who used gems in a method most-similar to today's crystal healing techniques. The Ancient Chinese had a special fascination with Jade, a green-colored stone which they believed held strong powers and embodied the five most important virtues they kept. For the Ancient Chinese, Jade symbolized courage, charity, justice, modesty, and wisdom.

Almost every ancient civilization believed in the powers of crystals. They attributed the luminous and colored stones they uncovered from the earth to specific characteristics, powers, and uses.

This fascination with stones continued until the 11th Century and the Renaissance Period. Publications about stones emerged. Experts conducted studies to prove that a crystal carried its own magical prowess. It was the time when books and writings about astrological works began to emerge. Writers began publishing manuals discussing different types of precious stones alongside the specific powers they carry, their specific uses, and the different illnesses they can heal.

Ancient cultures held on to the belief that crystals were special gifts sent by their gods. However, they also believed that crystals could be corrupted, especially when held by a sinner. This paved the way for the emergence of crystal cleansing techniques that are still widely practiced until this day.

During the Renaissance Period, people did not have access to proper medication and education. They simply relied on crystals to treat specific illnesses of the body, and even of the mind.

Modern Era of Crystals

Ancient civilizations strongly established the use and healing properties of crystals. Therefore, the incorporation of crystal healing in the early times of modern medicine should come as no surprise.

Crystals were important in Modern Indian society where people were taught about the importance of Nirvana. Indians used crystals for over-all mental and spiritual healing, along with other traditional medical techniques.

Aside from the Indian people, the Chinese also adopted the method of using stones for holistic wellness. They introduced the concept of chakras; declaring that the human body is capable of awakening a specific chakra by using a special energy-absorbing stone.

When the New Age started, Western people adopted these holistic concepts and began using stones as an over-all wellness method akin to today's crystal healing techniques.

In the 1980's, the demand for more knowledge about the mysteries of crystals grew higher. As a response, experts published more studies about the power of crystals. As more information and studies have been established, the practice of crystal healing has immensely flourished in the modern times. Many modern people use crystals not only for holistic wellness, but for other purposes like décor and jewelry as well.

To this day, the concept of using crystals continues to grow. Chakras are becoming a more widely accepted concept for example, and the demand for alternative therapies is growing steadily.

Many people, including some famous celebrities, are clinging onto crystals' magical abilities to enhance their lives. Popular American model Miranda Kerr has openly shared her ritual of placing a tiny chunk of Rose Quartz in her left brassiere. This pink crystal is known for opening up the heart chakra; therefore, attracting all forms of love.

Chapter 2: The Science of Crystal Healing

With the advancement of science and technology, a crystal's credibility has become more established. The basis of its healing and metaphysical properties are no longer just rooted from the beliefs and traditions imposed by ancient societies. The effect of crystal healing is now backed up by solid scientific evidence and data.

In 1913, Albert Einstein introduced the Theory of Zero Point Energy. Years later, with the widespread acceptance of crystal healing in modern society, experts used this theory to test the prowess of crystals. They developed a crystal-based machine that produces a stable electromagnetic field.

This electromagnetic field was tested over different types of liquid. The researchers found out that the electromagnetic field from crystals is ten times more capable of generating electricity. Through this study, it was also proven that a crystal's electromagnetic field is capable of inducing calmness and feelings of sensitivity, harnessing its effects on a person's mental state.

Crystals have a strong property called Piezoelectricity which is scientifically known to produce electricity from mechanical pressure. Therefore, a crystal can produce an electric charge when pressured, such as when compressed, or stretched.

In turn, this electric charge causes the crystal to vibrate as fast as 30,000 times per second. The human body, on the other hand, is scientifically known to regularly create electrical signals. Therefore, the relationship between the human body and crystals is scientifically undeniable.

The body's Central Nervous System has electric frequencies that run along the spine. When aligned with its set frequencies, the spine vibrates through its major energy centers. Connected to these major energy centers are specific nerve centers; the seven chakras, for example. Therefore, there is a strong connection between the Central Nervous System and vibrations. This connection provides one of the most solid foundations as to how crystals affect the body.

Crystals provide vibrations that the body can connect to. When in harmony, the body's energy centers can flow freely and be attuned to a frequency that is associated to a specific metaphysical or physical issue.

All crystals are composed of Oxygen and Silica, two of the most dominant elements on earth. This can be used as evidence that a crystal is one of the basic building blocks of life.

Eighty percent of the earth's crust is composed of Silica and Oxygen. Silicon is also a strong electricity conductor. This makes crystal an important element in both technology and nature.

Scientists have proven that the universe and everything in it, including the human body and solid materials like crystals, are made up of energies. They may be invisible to the naked eye, but researchers confirm that the human body and crystals are made up of just the same kind of energies.

Through modern advancements, scientists have already found ways of incorporating crystals in mankind's daily living. The watch you wear, for example, is composed of a clear Quartz crystal, which is responsible for making it work.

Crystals are even being used in modern medicine. Most pharmaceutical companies use grounded minerals found inside healing crystals when manufacturing medicines.

Other experts have tried testing the effects of crystal healing on animals in order to attain objective results. In a study done by crystal therapists, it was found out that animals also absorb electromagnetic energies from precious stones. A cat, for example, can sense the location of Amethysts placed on a cloth. The cat consistently goes over the Amethyst healing net to rest.

Crystal healing can also be applied to sick animals. If placing a crystal on the animal's body seems inconvenient, then, the animal can drink gem elixir instead.

The most common method of using a crystal for healing is placing it over the body to transfer energies. Crystals can transfer their healing properties akin to a magnet. When placed over a certain part of the body, the crystal allows the energies in the body to move, vibrate, pulse, and shift depending on the metaphysical properties enveloped in the crystal. It is believed that these energies are responsible for the body's overall wellness.

There is no limit to the kind of sickness or ailment that a crystal can heal. Its metaphysical and healing properties can be harnessed as long as you pick the right stone, and practice the right applications. Crystals can heal physical sicknesses from migraines to body aches. They can also heal emotional sickness like depression and anxiety. Further, crystals also promote holistic healing by balancing the body's seven chakras.

Adapted from the spiritual traditions of Eastern people, the body is composed of seven chakras that represent different life aspects. These include the physical, spiritual, psychological, and energetic elements of the body.

The first chakra is called Root which is located at the base of the spine. The second chakra is referred to as Sacral which is just beneath the navel. Known as Solar Plexus, the third chakra is located at the stomach. The fourth chakra is referred to as Heart, which is basically at the center of the chest. The fifth chakra is called Throat which is located at the base of the throat. Located at the small imaginary spot in the middle of the forehead and between the two eyes, the sixth chakra is referred to as Third Eye. The last chakra is called Crown, which is at the crown of the head. These chakras are not physical entities, but spiritual energies.

A crystal has three ways of healing and regulating the imbalance of energies in the body. The first method is called energizing in which a crystal transfers energy into the mind, body, and soul through the aid of frequencies. A crystal takes energy from its own quantum field and transfers it to your body's own energy field. This method is comparable to how electricity transfers and conducts energy to an object.

Clearing is the second method wherein the crystal acts like a magnet that picks up negative energies from the body.

Lastly, the balancing method deals primarily with one's inner peace. Cosmic experts say that the energies in the human body are symmetrical or in a perfect alignment. However, this alignment becomes irregular due to external factors like stress. A crystal can repel and attract the imbalanced energies in the body to promote internal harmony.

Chapter 3: How to Use Crystals for Self-Healing

Using crystals for healing is not limited only to placing them over the affected area of the body. Crystals are believed to also heal even when just worn, held, or placed in a special spot.

Placing the Crystals on the Body

The most common way of using a healing crystal is placing it over a specific area of the body. This technique is used in modern spa salons. It is effective when dealing with a specific tension in the body like a headache, or muscle spasms. Simply place the crystal on the affected area. If you are working on a specific chakra, choose a stone that complements that chakra, and place it on the body. The crystals will stir the energies in that specific body part to clear it of tension.

However, crystals do not have to just sit steady over the body. Moving the crystals around the body also holds a different type of power as the energy field in the body extends for up to 3ft around you. You may opt to use a crystal roller. A crystal roller looks like a handy wand with two stones on both ends. The tool works smoothly like a small paint roller. Simply glide the stones across different parts of the body to balance your entire aura.

In the beauty department, Rose Quartz rollers have become a trend. Since Rose Quartz has a soft pink shade, a lot of women have become fascinated with its alluring beauty. A Rose Quartz roller is used to glide over the face in order to heal skin impurities.

Using the crystals in meditation

By simply holding a powerful and energetic stone during a quiet meditation, you can begin to experience serene moments of insightful and life-changing calmness. To apply this technique, the first step is to look for a peaceful spot away from external distractions. Next, hold a crystal in your hands. Close your eyes and focus on your breathing. Breathe in deeper for the first few seconds to release tension in the mind and body.

As you relax more, focus on lighter, but steady breaths. Let the crystals resonate around you. You may feel as light as a feather, or as if you are floating in the air. Sometimes, you may also feel like your body is sinking deep into the earth. There are also others who say that meditating with crystals gives them an unexplainable feeling of goosebumps.

There might also be times when a crystal does not give a resonating sensation. It may simply mean that the crystal you are holding gives off a different vibration and is not suitable for your needs or intentions. When this happens, just be patient and experiment with another crystal, as every stone carries a unique metaphysical property.

Sleeping with a Crystal around You

Sleeping with a crystal near you will aid in healing and repelling negativities in your subconscious mind. These negativities are mostly fears that the rational mind is trying to ignore, and often translate into nightmares. Waking up sluggish is a clear sign that your subconscious mind is disrupted with negativities.

A person's mind is dominated by inner hurdles when at rest. Therefore, the best time to heal the misalignment of mental energies is during sleep. You may put a crystal under your pillow, beside you, or in a spot near you. The crystal will clear the subconscious mind from all the negativities overnight. This results in you feeling more recharged and positive upon waking up in the morning. More so, some people even notice the crystal's positive effects on their dreams.

Create a Crystal Grid

A single crystal held in one hand already holds incredible powers. Yet, you may still multiply these powers a hundred times by aligning different crystals together in a grid.

Creating a crystal grid is an ancient practice of arranging numerous crystals in a harmonic geometrical pattern to combine all their powers. This is especially suitable if you are trying to achieve a specific intention.

This concept is comparable to a typical football game scenario. A single player may be strong on his own, but as he joins forces with other teammates, the combined strengths and abilities create more power.

Each crystal has different external energies that revolve around it in various forms such as electromagnetism, sound, and light. When combined with others, the crystals are unified into a universal force.

To make a crystal grid, first, direct your mind to a specific goal. You will be asking the crystals to work on this goal for you. It may be a specific dream that you want to attract, or an illness that you want to be healed of; just be specific about it. Aside from the manner of aligning the crystals, a clear intention is also a powerful element that can strengthen the crystals' energies. Write this intention on a piece of paper. Keep in mind that the crystals have the power to attract anything you declare and ask from the universe.

Then, choose the crystals for your grid. You may opt for a crystal that complements your intention, for example, a Rose Quartz if you intend to attract love and inner peace. Basically, there are no rules when choosing the crystals. You may simply let your intuition guide you and pick whatever you wish.

After choosing the crystals, cleanse them and the spot where you intend to place the grid. There are numerous methods used in cleansing and charging the crystals. Washing them under running water or submerging in a salt solution are the most common cleansing methods. However, be careful in doing these as not all crystals can be submerged in water. These methods require thorough research on a crystal's physical components. In order to be safe, you may opt for other cleansing techniques like moon bathing, sunlight bathing, smudging, or burying.

Next, place the piece of paper (where you wrote your intention) in the middle of your chosen sacred space. This step is a key element in making a crystal grid; therefore, it requires deep concentration. Slowly declare your intentions either mentally or by saying them aloud. While declaring the intention, make an effort to connect with your inner mind and the universe. You may even play soothing music or light a candle to immerse yourself in the ritual.

Then, lay each crystal down on the grid; making a specific pattern or alignment. A usual crystal grid is composed of one Focus Stone in the center; surrounded by six Way Stones, and another set of six Destination Stones.

The Focus Stone serves as the magnet that amplifies and attracts the Central Life Force through the powers of its energy lattice. Then, it scatters the Central Life Force to the other stones in an inward and downward flowing wave.

The Way Stones, or the crystals surrounding the Focus Stone, are important elements in the grid. Their responsibility is comparable to a water pump that modifies and amplifies the water flowing down the pipe. The Way Stones also amplify the universal energy flowing from the Focus Stone and scatter it further throughout the grid.

The Destination Stones, or the outermost layers of crystals, represent the end goal or purpose of the grid. These stones must be chosen based on the grid's final intention. These crystals gather the energies from the Focus Stones and Way Stones; and mold them into the desired intention of the grid.

The lines or path of energies complement the design of the grid. Every grid comes in different geometric shapes, and each shape has its own significant spiritual meaning. The lines in the grid serve as the pathways of energy, guiding the stones on the journey towards the intention. They transmit and align the energies into your desired intention.

One of the most commonly used geometric shapes in a crystal grid is the Flower of Life. It has nineteen circles that overlap

each other; creating a pattern of flowers. There is a large circle
that surrounds the nineteen overlapping ones. The Flower of
Life is a strong universal symbol of nature, life, and all creations
in the universe. This symbol resembles the essential creations
on earth - fruit, flowers, snowflakes, and human cells. It is
believed to have a strong connection to the energies beyond the
physical realm.

Another common grid pattern is the Borromean Rings. At a
glance, the Borromean Rings look like three overlapping ovals.
This pattern originated from Celtic mythology; symbolizing their
Moon Goddess. The trinity is also attributed to the harmony of
the mind, body, and spirit.

Other common patterns of sacred geometry used in a crystal
grid are Mandela, The Eye of Horus, Hexagon, Pentagon,
Square, Circle, Triangle, and the Seed of Life.

You can hold a crystal wand and close your eyes as you travel
your mind into the galaxies. Believe that pulses of life energy
and pure love are flowing from the galaxy into the wand. Point
the wand at the Focus Stone. Imagine that the pulses of life
energy from the wand are being streamed out into the Focus
Stone. Then, point the wand to each crystal; creating an
imaginary line that connects the crystals to each other.
Remember that the person who declared the intention must also

be the one to complete this step. If the intention is for a group of people, then everyone must join in the aligning ritual.

When you have the time to stop by your grid every day, spend a few moments attracting all the energies flowing from the crystals. Allow these energies to guide you towards your intentions or desires.

Wear Your Crystals

During the ancient times, crystals were worn by high priests and queens through their breast plates and crowns. Wearing a crystal as jewelry can help in balancing your energy levels throughout the day. Remember that crystals can repel, absorb, and transmit energy around them. Adorning your body with a crystal works similarly to taking a supplement in the morning. The pill works by nourishing the body all throughout the day. The crystal also works the same way by nourishing your energy levels.

You may also carry a healing crystal with you. However, keeping the crystal hidden such as putting it in your pocket is not advisable. Any form of clothing can shield the energies absorbed by the crystal. As much as possible, the crystal must have direct contact with the skin.

If you cannot avoid putting the crystal in your pockets or wallet, you may simply bring it out whenever you need to. American singer Adele admits holding a healing stone in her hand to fight and calm down her stage fright when performing. As a bonus, wearing the crystal as jewelry makes you look more enticing and attractive as crystals have an undeniable allure.

Use It as a Decor

Crystal decors can jazz up your space, add a luxurious feeling to your home, and bring about holistic healing. Decorating your home with healing stones can strengthen your connection with Mother Nature. In turn, it can bring peace, therapeutic benefit, and calmness to your inner self.

Healing crystals can also attract abundance and repel negative energies. Nowadays, crystal decors have been jazzed up to suit modern architectural designs. Since crystal gardening is becoming a trend today, air plants mounted on a crystal are now one of modern architecture's top choices for decors. Crystals hanged in a dream catcher can also be displayed on a wall. Crystallized lighting also adds gorgeous and elegant appeal to a space. Some examples of crystallized lighting are lampshades, pendant lights, or chandeliers encrusted with gem stones.

Drink a Gem Essence

A gem essence, also known as a gem elixir, or crystal water, can also be mixed into your drinking water. Making a gem elixir is akin to the process of making a flower essence. You may use a single crystal or a combination of different types in making an elixir. Using more crystals, of course, brings a more powerful synergy blend.

Prepare the following ingredients and materials:

1. One or more crystals whose energy you want to absorb. As a tip, adding one Clear Quartz can bring stronger energy charge to the elixir.

2. Two dark-colored glass bottles of different sizes; brown or dark blue is best.

3. Two clean ceramic containers of different sizes. The smaller container must fit inside the larger one. It is recommended to use a deep ceramic bowl and one smaller clear glass or jar.

4. One dropper.

5. Preservative – this can be any variety of vinegar or vodka. This will also be used to establish the energy vibrations of the crystals.

6. Distilled or spring water. Others prefer using rain water to make the gem essence more attuned to the universe.

7. A sacred space – this can be indoors if you like, but it's best if it can also be an area that gets direct sunlight or moon light; such as a place by a window.

Follow these steps in making the elixir or gem essence:

1. Clear or charge the crystals.

2. Choose a spot with abundant sunlight or moonlight. You may also opt for your personal sacred space.

3. Once you are ready to make the gem essence, clear and align your mind to the universe. You can meditate, pray, or take controlled breaths. Then, declare your intention to the universe. You must have a specific intention that the gem essence will work on. Embrace divine assistance and the aid of crystals in declaring your intentions.

4. Put the crystals in the smaller container (the clear glass or jar). Seal the container if possible.

5. Place the smaller container inside the larger one (deep ceramic bowl). Slowly pour the water in the larger container. Be sure that the water will not get inside the small container.

6. Surround the container with additional crystals to intensify the energy.

7. Again, state your intentions aloud.

8. Leave the set-up under the sunlight, moonlight, or in a sacred space for five hours or more. This will allow the water to absorb all the energies from the crystals.

9. Once ready, carefully take the small container out. The charged water in the deeper bowl is called the Mother Essence, or Stock. Get a large bottle and fill it with ¾ of the stock.

10. Add the vinegar or vodka in the large bottle and seal it. The vodka or vinegar will act as a preservative. When refrigerated, the gem essence will last for a few days.

9. Pour the remaining stock or mother essence into the smaller bottle and drink it immediately. If you want to dilute the stock first, you may simply add a little distilled or spring water.

Chapter 4: Using Crystals to Heal Others

Crystal Therapy

Crystal Therapy is the healing technique of placing different minerals or crystals on a person's body. This helps them let go of stress and pain, acquire a deep state of relaxation, and balance the energies in the body. The crystals are placed on the meridian or acupuncture points, painful spots in the body, or on the chakras. Sometimes, the crystals are not placed on the body itself, but around the patient instead.

This technique is commonly used in spa treatments or healing salons and is done by crystal therapists bearing a professional certification. It can also be done by anyone as long as he/she is equipped with sufficient knowledge in crystal healing.

There are several factors to consider in crystal therapy such as the type of illness or pain and the metaphysical properties of a chosen stone. You can rely on your intuition in deciding where to place the crystals. However, professional crystal therapists use a specific layout when placing the crystals on the patient's body.

One of the most common layouts used in crystal therapy is called "The figure of eight". In this layout, the crystals are arranged to form a figure similar to the number eight (8). It is used to release stagnant energies in a specific area of the body.

Another common layout is called the "Seal of Solomon". In this layout, six crystals are used to form a star figure. A crystal in the center is optional but can bring more intense healing. The "Seal of Solomon" is especially used to relieve stress and pain.

The layout or position of the crystals depends on the patient's pain. Professional crystal healers believe that a particular pain in the body is simply an external manifestation of an internal energy misalignment.

For example, crystal therapists say that a headache is simply caused by a blockage in the body's energy. When healing a headache, Amethyst has the greatest ability to move the blocked energy into proper alignment.

To begin, let the patient lie on their back. Put two crystals on the throat with the pointed side facing upwards. The crystals must be aligned with both innermost ends of the collarbones.

Use another crystal and place it above the crown of the head; with the pointed side facing away from the crown. Rest the last crystal on the forehead's middle point; or the brow chakra. The pointed side of the crystal must be facing upwards towards the crown of the head.

If the patient complains of a headache rooted from the neck muscles, then place another crystal on the neck's cervical vertebrae just below the back of the head. The crystal's pointed side must be facing towards the head. You may use a micropore to help the crystal stay in place.

Sore Throat

A few of the underlying illnesses related to a sore throat can be laryngitis, thyroid problems, mouth ulcers, pain in the ear, and difficulty hearing.

The throat chakra is associated with self-knowledge, willpower, making sound choices and getting in touch with one's inner truth. Therefore, a blockage in the throat chakra hinders the mind's ability to make important decisions and transformational actions.

Perfectly aligned energies in the throat chakra promote the courage to make powerful decisions, and the will to embrace unchangeable things. A well-balanced throat chakra allows a person to freely and honestly express his/her beliefs.

The "Star of Solomon" is the most common layout used when healing an ailment related to the throat. Place one crystal at the base of the throat; just above the dip between the inner corners of the collar bones. Then, place six or eight other stones around the base crystal. Place another crystal below the star-shaped layout; just above the upper base of the chest. Lastly, place another crystal at the lower base of the chest.

Stress

Stress and other related problems are becoming more prevalent in today's fast-paced society. To heal stress using crystals, you will need seven crystal points. However, instead of resting the crystals on the body, you will have to place them on the mat (where the patient is lying down) instead.

First, place one crystal above the head. Next, place another set of crystals on both sides of the shoulders. Place the next crystals on both sides of the knees. Lastly, place two crystals below the feet. The pointed sides of the crystals must be facing upward. Let the patient relax for four to five minutes. After five minutes, let the crystals face inwards (towards the body). Wait for another four or five minutes and return the crystals into their original position (facing upwards). Do this alternately.

Using a Crystal Roller for Body Massage

One of the most recent trends in today's modern era of crystal healing is the emergence of a handy gem tool called a crystal roller. This wellness gizmo looks like a small wand or paint roller. Its handle is also made of crystal, and attached on both ends are two stones of different sizes. One end is a larger and rounder crystal that is meant to be rolled on the plumper areas of the body. On the other end is a smaller and flatter stone that is meant to be glided on small joints and corners of the body. Initially, these rollers began as a tool for facial massage, but have slowly evolved into a versatile tool to relieve body aches.

The concept of using a crystal roller is linked to the scientific flow of the body's lymphatic system. The lymphatic system is considered as the body's waste area where toxins and all other impurities are collected. Ideally, these impurities must be flushed out of the body. However, unlike the circulatory system which has the heart as its pump, the lymphatic system does not have its own pump. It does not have the ability to flush out the collected toxins by itself. Its performance relies on your own actions – by having an active lifestyle, and engaging in physical activities.

When the lymphatic system is clogged due to a poor lifestyle, the collected toxins and impurities will be stocked inside the human body. This eventually results in poor immunity and frequent sickness. Gliding a crystal roller over the lymph nodes can help ease blockages and flush impurities out of the system.

Using a Crystal Roller to Massage the Arms

There are no golden rules to follow when using a crystal roller for massage. You may simply glide the roller depending on the person's mood. The number of strokes or length of each session solely depends on you and the patient.

A good way to begin is to glide the crystal roller from the armpit down the elbow using gentle pressure and slow strokes. Roll from the elbow going up to the shoulder. Next, massage the lower arm by rolling from the elbow until you reach the wrist.

If the patient complains of nerve illnesses such as carpal tunnel syndrome, focus on massaging the plump side of the lower arm. Glide the roller from the wrist to the elbows in back-and-forth motions. Doing this repetitively can tear down scar tissue and adhesions in the wrist and forearm muscles. As a result, symptoms of carpal tunnel syndrome are also broken down.

Using a Crystal Roller to Massage the Legs

Begin by massaging the groin area down into the thighs. Roll diligently on the thighs. Next, move down to the lower leg, making downward rolls starting from the back of the knee. The downward strokes in the lower leg can aid in the proper drainage of the lymphatic system. If there is an injured area in the leg, massaging with a crystal roller can make the recovery faster. It can also reduce the bruising and swelling. Crystal roller massage is also recommended to patients who have recently had knee surgeries.

Using a Crystal Roller to Massage the Breasts

Under scientific lenses, the anatomy of breasts is composed of root-like structures called lymph nodes. These lymph nodes are scattered around the breastbone, armpits, and upper and lower quadrants of the breast. Therefore, the breast is susceptible to clogging of toxins and impurities, especially for those who have a poor lifestyle and inadequate levels of physical activity. When neglected, the clogging of toxins in the breast area can lead to serious diseases.

Massaging the breast should be part of anyone's daily health routine. To begin, ask the patient to lie down on their back. Roll the crystal over the inner side of the nipple going to the breastbone using light circular motions. Next, go over the breast's upper quadrant and roll going to the armpit. Then, using horizontal strokes, massage the lower quadrant of the breast.

Using a Crystal Roller to Massage the Foot

A crystal roller can be used to lessen the swelling of the feet. It is also a perfect way to pamper the feet after a long and tiring day. This tool can even be incorporated in a foot spa or pedicure session. With gentle motions, massage the ball of the foot. From the ball of the foot, roll down to the heel with firm downward strokes. Repeat as you wish.

Chapter 5: Proper Cleansing, Recharging, and Storing

Cleansing the Crystals

Just like the human body, crystals can also be dull and drained of energy. Cleansing a crystal must be done regularly in order to send it to its highest and purest spiritual form. Crystals used in healing are more prone to absorbing negative energies. When left uncleansed, the crystal's healing powers may be lessened. Fortunately, there are several ways of cleansing a crystal, and they are all quite therapeutic as well!

Cleansing with Salt Water

Salt is known for having strong cleansing properties, and is one of the most common ingredients used in crystal cleansing. To apply this method, fill a ceramic bowl with a salt solution. Sea salt is recommended but if it is not available, regular cooking salt can be an option. Submerge the crystals in the bowl of salt solution for a day or more. The more used the crystal is, the more cleansing it needs. Some people even submerge their crystals for a week. After submerging in the salt solution, wash the crystals under running water to remove the remaining salt that may be stuck to the gem. Never recycle the used salt water as it has already absorbed the unwanted and negative energies from the crystals.

However, there are several crystals that are not suitable for salt water. Gems that have water and metal content are not recommended to be cleansed using this method. The salt water may just destroy the crystal's appearance and negatively affect its powers. Examples of these gems are Lapis Lazuli, Opal, Hematite, and Pyrite.

Cleansing with Dry Salt

Another way of cleansing a crystal is placing it in a bowl of pure salt. Again, sea salt is the best option, but regular cooking salt will also do just fine. You may either submerge the crystal completely under the salt, or you may just rest them on the surface. Then, leave the crystal for 24 hours, or even seven days if you wish, depending on the amount of impurities it has absorbed. Again, be careful not to use this method with porous gems or those that have water or metal content.

If you think you have a porous crystal but still want to use salt as a cleansing ingredient, then you may follow this method. First, put dry salt in a bowl or a large glass. Again, you may choose between sea salt and regular cooking salt. Then, take a smaller glass and bury it in the bowl of salt. Place the crystals inside the empty smaller glass. Despite not being in direct contact with the salt, the crystals will still be cleansed. The salt can still absorb all the impurities from the stones. However, this technique may take longer to take full effect.

You may also take a little amount of pure, mineral or distilled water and pour it over the smaller glass with just enough to cover the crystals. This method will reduce the chances of the crystals being in direct contact with the salt.

Cleansing through Smudging

Smudging is also a common method of cleansing the energy field of crystals. It is the method of using the smoke of burning herbs to purify crystals and clear them of negative energies. First, choose the herbs that you want to use. White sage is the most common herb used in smudging as it is scientifically known to release negative ions in space. Sage will not only cleanse the crystal itself, but its environment as well. You may also combine it with lavender. Sweet grass and Yerba Santa can be used as well.

Next, tie the bundle of herbs together to create a stick and allow it to dry. There are also several crystal stores that sell pre-bundled herbal sticks. Treat the smudge stick with deep respect as it is considered sacred, especially when used in rituals of spiritual purification.

Once the herbal stick begins to burn, gently fan it using a feather. If a feather is not available, you may simply blow the herbal stick. Then, let the smoke surround the crystal. If a smudging stick is not available, you may use incense but make sure that it is made of natural materials and is free from toxic chemicals.

Cleansing through Visualization

The visualization method is a simple way of cleansing and recharging a crystal. Yet, it requires a deep connection with one's imagination. You must possess the ability to visually see what you are imagining in order to successfully perform this method.
Your heart must also be at peace; focusing only on your intentions.

To do this method, visualize that there are rays of light shining above the crystals; as if the light is a spiritual guide coming from the heavens. Also, visualize that the crystals are surrounded by a beam of white light. Then, believe that the lights are taking the negativities and impurities from the crystals. Continue doing this until you finally see and feel that the crystals have been cleansed.

Recharging the Crystal

There is a difference between simply cleansing a crystal and recharging it. Cleansing a crystal is removing all the negative energies that it has absorbed throughout its usage. Recharging, on the other hand, is actually imbuing it with positive energies, feelings, and vibrations. Therefore, after cleansing the crystal, it is also necessary to recharge it until it becomes ready for the next use.

Recharging through Sunlight and Moonlight Bathing

Placing the crystals under sunlight or moonlight will give them positive vibrations. Both sunlight and moonlight give off strong energies. However, it is said that the sun is more powerful than the moon. Others take advantage of their combined powers.

To begin, wash the crystals and pat them dry. Bring them out to the earth for a moon bath first; ideally, just after sunset. Ideally, the crystals must be placed on a natural surface. You may also lay them in a crystal grid if you want to.

This method is best done under a full moon as it is said to have deep restorative energy. Let the crystals stay under the moonlight until the next sunrise. Just remember not to let the crystals stay under the sunlight for too long to avoid the fading of colors.

Clouds do not bring any effect to the crystal's energy. You may apply the moon bathing method even if it is raining or overcast. Just be sure not to bathe crystals that are not suitable for water. Some examples of crystals that are not suitable for water are Malachite and Selenite.

Recharging by Rubbing with the Hands

Purifying the stones can also be done by rubbing them with your palms or by simply holding them. In this method, you will act as the spiritual guide who will direct the crystals in releasing all their negative energies.

As a spiritual guide, your mind and body must be cleansed first. Wash your hair and body and put on a clean set of clothes. Clear your mind from all distractions and negative thoughts; focus only on your intentions with the crystals. You must also look for a clutter-free space. This way, you will be able to guide the stones on a smooth journey.

Storing the Crystal

Your crystals can still strengthen your vibes and aura even when they are not in use. Proper storage can not only deepen the crystals' powers but also deepen your bond with them. It also protects them from dust, preventing damage.

There are many types of materials used in storing crystals such as glass cases, silk pouches, wooden boxes, safety lock bags, and geodes. According to many cosmic enthusiasts, silk and handwoven cloths are the best place for resting a crystal. Be sure not to place the crystals under direct sunlight for a long time as doing so can fade their colors.

If you have several types of crystals and you want to keep them organized, you may group them according to color, chakra association, or sizes. Although, the best way to organize crystals is according to their physical attributes – sizes and shapes – because crystals can chip and scratch themselves when grouped inappropriately. For example, crystals with sharp edges can scratch other crystals with fragile and smooth surfaces.

Chapter 6: Choosing the Right Crystal

Out of thousands of crystals available on earth, how do you find one that suits your needs and personality? Remember that you, as an individual entity in the universe, have your own vibrations. There are certain crystals that will work well for you, and some that will not gravitate towards your vibrational frequencies.

Picking up a crystal that does not suit your vibrations is perfectly fine. You simply have to try again on the next one. After all, cosmic healers say that you do not choose the right crystal, but the right crystal chooses you. Just like in any other things in life, choosing a crystal may take a little patience on your part.

When in limbo, seek help from the universe. Asking guidance from the universe is the first thing that cosmic healers do. If you are a firm believer of the universe's abilities to shower you with signs, then you may consider taking this step. Conducting full research about a crystal's metaphysical properties is not a requirement in this technique. You just have to simply trust that the universe will deliver the right stone for you.

Asking guidance from the universe is not complicated at all. You simply have to ask for signs through meditation, deep thoughts, and prayers. Trust that the universe has a deep respect for your spiritual powers and is always listening.

Another way of choosing the best crystal is by observing how your soul reacts to it. Take a feel of the stone's vibrations in your hands. Gently squeeze the crystal and observe if it brings you emotional or physical sensations. Observe if the crystal has a tantalizing effect on you. This may bring you a sense of feeling energized, heat, or tranquility.

Chapter 7: Crystals and Their Powers

In this chapter, you will find a comprehensive list of different types of crystals alongside the powers and healing abilities they possess. Every crystal is unique and equipped with different energies and properties. When choosing the right one, consider your personal intentions for using the crystal.

Despite their powers, the crystals discussed in this chapter are not rare. They can be easily found and more importantly, are not very expensive.

These crystals are categorized based on their colors. Identifying a crystal's color will help you determine which chakra it is associated with; giving you an easier analysis as to whether a crystal is best for physical, emotional, or spiritual healing.

Crystals and Their Powers Based on Colors

Blue Crystals

As calm and soothing as they are to the eyes, blue crystals are associated with the healing of emotional and physical energy misalignments. Representing the tranquility of the sky, ocean, and water, Blue Crystals are said to possess the serenity of the heavens. These gems are especially effective in healing stress and anxiety. They also promote relaxation and free communication; the ability to accept things as they are, contrary to today's hectic culture of forcing things due to people's impatience.

Angelite – as a stone for the heart chakra, Angelite is good for healing energy imbalances in the thyroid. It also reduces pain, especially if due to sunburn. Taking cue from its name, this stone opens up your deeper connection to your guardian angels. Therefore, it promotes peace and forgiveness while lowering the body's tension and stress. It is also great for people dealing with anger management problems.

Blue Lace Agate - this gem aids in the healing of respiratory and throat problems. This stone is also recommended for mental healing. Due to its blue color, it gives off calming and soothing vibrations that promote mental peacefulness. It is good in healing stress and anxiety.

Blue Apatite – this gem increases metabolism; therefore, it is suitable for people who are experiencing weight-loss problems. It has overall effects on the healing of the organs and glands in the body. Known as a strong inspirational crystal, Blue Apatite boosts mental creativity and promotes mental clarity.

Celestite – in terms of physical healing, Celestite removes toxins from the body that are caused by tension and stress. It aids in the healing of digestive disorders and other illnesses like fever and infection. Celestite protects the intestines from parasites that also cause infection. It also heals problems related to the eyes, ears, and throat. It is a spiritual stone that helps fight sadness, anxiety, and other heavy moods. It has a gentle and uplifting vibration. It is also believed to attract angels around you.

Chrysocolla – Chrysocolla is best for the healing of illnesses related to the larynx and throat. It aids in the good performance of adrenals and the thyroid. This gem is recommended to pregnant women as it promotes a happy pregnancy, especially during the crucial first trimester period. It also eases the pain experienced during menstruation. It heals pain and problems related to the hips and hip joints. The abilities to express one's self and, clearly communicate are two of the strongest spiritual benefits of Chrysocolla. It is also soothing and promotes mental peacefulness. It brings relaxation and calmness during periods of change and transition. It can also bring love into your life.

Dumortierite – this crystal is commonly used by crystal healers in treating epilepsy and hypersensitivity. It also heals ailments related to the thyroid and parathyroid area, as well as skin disorders including sunburn. This stone is also used in the treatment of intestinal problems including diarrhea and stomach ache. It relieves headaches, nausea, cramping, vomiting, as well as negative symptoms of pregnancy. This crystal is also intended for the third eye chakra. It gives overflowing patience, willpower and insight. Dumortierite is the stone of intellect; it especially improves one's mathematical and language abilities.

Labradorite - Labradorite cleanses the body from toxins. This stone is best for women who are suffering from hormonal imbalance. It is also recommended for those who have poor heart health. Labradorite is a gem of power and destiny. It can help you transform into the person that you are destined to be. It helps give an overflowing energy supply, and protects your overall aura by acting as an energy shield.

Lapis Lazuli – Lapis Lazuli helps induce a well-rested sleep; making you happier and more recharged for the next day. It has good healing properties including the treatment of headache, vertigo, body pains, and PMS. It is a gem of insight, awareness and truth. Lapis Lazuli is a protection and manifestation stone; helping you turn your dreams into reality.

Ocean Jasper - Ocean Jasper is helpful in maintaining the proper balance of iodine and sodium levels in the body. It helps the body absorb more vitamins and minerals. It also aids in the drainage of the lymphatic system, and restores tissues in the internal organs. Ocean Jasper also helps in the relieving of water retention in the body. This crystal can bring you into a state of genuine bliss. It lifts the spirit and calms the mind and body to encourage joy at the present moment.

Peacock ore - Known as the "Stone of the Mystic", Peacock Ore has the rare ability of helping you find missing objects. It is believed to aid in developing someone's inner vision. It is often paired with healing techniques like acupressure and acupuncture. Peacock Ore eases pressure caused by tumors, and restores the body's DNA. It can also heal contagious respiratory diseases. It encourages new ideas and strengthens creative energies. Peacock Ore is also a crystal of happiness, creativity, blessings, and innovation.

Sodalite - This gem has tranquil and balancing effects on the body because of its high content of calcium, manganese, and salt. It is the crystal for inspiration, confidence, intuition and communication.

Turquoise - Turquoise is a crystal for the throat chakra that promotes communication rooted from honesty and the heart's true desires and intentions. It has vibrational powers that serve as a deep connection between the sky, heaven, and earth. These powers make it known as the master healer.

Black Crystals

Black crystals are linked to power, mystery, and protection. Mankind is used to associating black with fear and the unknown. Representing the color of the night sky during the absence of the star's illumination, black is often feared and believed to be a color of bad luck. For the longest time, people have associated black with death and danger. Yet, cosmic enthusiasts believe that black is actually a positive color. Many amulets come in the color of black as it actually represents protection or being hidden from one's enemies. Black crystals are also associated with the root chakra.

Basalt - this crystal is created from the cooled basaltic lava of a volcano. It is a dark volcanic crystal that increases the body's energy levels. It also encourages stability and courage; hence, it was given the nickname "spiritual cheerleader". Basalt is a strong spiritual guide. Living with the trace of the intense power of volcanoes, this stone has already gained a lot of experience under the earth. It has undergone transformations over time. Therefore, Basalt is the stone of wisdom. It encourages you to be a warrior of the universe; journeying in the pursuit of happiness.

Black Kyanite - this balancing stone can heal misalignments in the chakras by releasing blockages in each center. It is good for energy protection and clearing out things that are no longer connected with your highest spiritual reality. Known as the

Revival Stone, Black Kyanite cleanses the body from negative energies and replaces them with positive ones.

Black Obsidian – in terms of physical healing, Black Obsidian is the gem for fighting digestive problems. It also helps lower blood pressure, heals ailments in the gall bladder, and improves the condition of the heart. It also aids in fighting against viral infections and contributes to the strengthening of the muscle tissues. Black Obsidian is the gem of truth; giving you the ability to discern the deepest mysteries of the people around you, and life in general. This stone has a strong vibration that can awaken someone's spirituality. It helps clear your overall aura by connecting you to the earth's vibrations and eliminating negativities. Psychic protection can also be given by a Black Obsidian.

Rainbow Obsidian - this crystal heals the heart, not just from its physical ailments but most especially from its traumatic experiences. This stone is best for people who are suffering from emotional pain such as when experiencing death of a loved one, or a break-up. It cleanses the overall emotional state of the body.

Black Onyx - A protective and powerful stone, Black Onyx has mental healing properties. It can calm down your fears by protecting your body, mind, and spirit from negative energies. As a result, you will feel more safe and secure.

Black Tourmaline - Its healing properties include reducing the symptoms and pain in the muscular system. It also heals spinal and intestinal problems. It can fight allergy attacks and protect you from harmful radiation which can be caught from electronic gadgets. Black Tourmaline is a strong crystal for holistic wellness. Black Tourmaline protects the over-all balance of energies in the chakras. It releases blockages of energies in the body.

Indigo Gabbro - Indigo Gabbro can be used to heal heart-related ailments. It is also said to heal sprains and bruises. It is an intuitive and magical gem that aligns your energies to the core of the earth; thus, promoting mental focus and helping drive away distractions. These metaphysical properties make it known as the "Wise Stone". Indigo Gabbro is also a spiritual stone that helps you align to the spiritual realm. Therefore, this gem is good for meditation.

Nuummite – Nuummite is recommended to those who suffer from diabetes. It is good for insulin production and regulation. It is also recommended to those who have low blood pressure and blood sugar. This gem is also good for healing insomnia. Nuummite also clears the outside energies to cleanse the inner energy field. Nuummite is one of the oldest stones on earth; existing for over three-billion years.

<u>Brown Crystals</u>

With their earthy vibes, brown crystals are known for absorbing negative energies from the body. Representing visually all kinds of life on earth, brown crystals will help you connect more to others; giving you the prowess to understand other people's situations and plights. It promotes a stronger sense of awareness in the world that you are living in. Brown crystals are also for security and stability.

Carnelian – this gem increases fertility and promotes good the function of the reproductive organs of both males and females. Carnelian also promotes good blood supply to the tissues and organs. It aids in metabolism and can ease the symptoms of menstrual cramps. It helps in the healing of rheumatism, arthritis, and back problems. This crystal has numerous benefits as it targets the first three chakras in the body. Therefore, it helps promote overflowing creative energies, boosts confidence and sexuality, and strengthens vitality and courage.

Jasper – patients who suffer from tissue deterioration can benefit from the healing properties of Jasper. It also heals ailments related to the spleen, kidneys, liver, bladder, and stomach. Jasper also balances the body's minerals such as zinc, iron, manganese, and sulfur. It is known as the symbol of the blood of the earth. It can bring you into a deeper connection with nature.

Smoky Quartz – a stone that is naturally irradiated, Smoky Quartz contradicts the effects of radiation. Therefore, it aids in the healing of sunburn and may also be good for those undergoing chemotherapy. It is a stabilizing gem that heals the heart and mind from negative energies such as jealousy, stress, fear, and anger.

Yellow and Gold Crystals

These colors will remind you of the sun during its most powerful time – midday. Yellow and gold crystals bring a little sunshine into your life by being the stones of joy and optimism. Yellow and gold crystals are associated with the solar plexus and sacral chakras. They are the stones for sexuality, willpower, and emotions. They promote confidence and comfort in your own abilities and creativity. They will help you transform from being just a timid follower to a strong leader. They are also the stones for clarity and purpose; helping you see things from a lighter and brighter perspective. With yellow and gold crystals, you will greet each day feeling refreshed and filled with optimism and zest.

Citrine – Citrine is good for strengthening the body's physical energy and stamina. It is recommended to people who are suffering from Chronic Fatigue Syndrome. It stimulates digestion and encourages proper metabolism. It also relieves skin allergies and irritations, especially if caused by food intolerance. This stone also maintains the health of hair, skin, and nails. Citrine is included in the list of crystals with zero negative energy. It is a stone that encourages abundance, happiness, light, and manifestation.

Pyrite - known as the Fool's Gold, Pyrite has a bright metallic shine. It has the ability to cleanse the oxygen circulating in the body; promoting good over-all performance of the cardiovascular system. It helps strengthen memory and provides help to those suffering from cognitive disorders and learning disabilities. Physically, this crystal's surface has a clear reflection that acts as a shield from negative energies. It attracts wealth, prosperity, and success.

Mookaite – in terms of physical healing, Mookaite prevents the deterioration of internal organs and helps restore tissues. It helps in the healing of ailments related to the digestive system, kidney, and bladder. It comes in different colors which are all earthy and vibrant. Mookaite helps you overcome your comfort zone and awakens your adventurous side. It is called as the "Gem of then and now"; helping you to be grateful of the past, enjoy the present, and hope for the future.

Tiger's Eye – This crystal is used in healing problems related to the endocrine system and is able to restore the body's biochemistry balance. Since it is a stone associated with the light of the sun, it is recommended to those who are prone to nightmares. Tiger's Eye heals the pessimistic aspects of a person, and increases their feelings of positivity. It is a solar gem for will, personal power, strength, and courage. Therefore, it also helps attract wealth, prosperity, and opportunities.

Green Crystals

Stones with green colors have balancing and healing effects on people's emotions, since they are crystals of the heart chakra. The color green is associated with wealth, abundance, and prosperity. Representing the colors of nature's energies and the beauty of life; green crystals promote growth, harmony, balance, and learning. They are considered as master healers and are very safe. Therefore, if you are not sure which crystals to choose, you may always opt first for a green stone as it is considered an all-around gem.

Chrysoprase — Believed to be the stone of Greek Goddess Aphrodite, Chrysoprase brings strong benefits to the heart chakra. It encourages opening up of the heart to let love come in. It also attracts optimism, joy and happiness. It promotes self-love, self-growth, empathy, and forgiveness.

Fuchsite — Known as the Healer's Stone, Fuchsite has tons of healing properties. It heals migraines, motions sickness, vertigo, and other related diseases. It strengthens the immune system. It can act as a natural pain reliever for some conditions such as muscle problems, spinal misalignment, and carpal tunnel syndrome. Fuchsite is one of the most favorite gems of women because of its flecks that resemble fairy dust. Its gold and green sparkle made it known as the "Fairy Crystal". Fuchsite can open up the heart for a deeper experience of love. It encourages relaxation, joyfulness, and miracles. Fuchsite is the gem for renewal and rejuvenation. It helps you attract a fresher perspective in life and approach things with excitement.

Aventurine - this stone is not known for its healing properties of physical, mental, or spiritual illnesses. Yet, a lot of enthusiasts and patients still choose aventurine as part of their rituals as it is known to intensify one's luck. It specifically attracts more prosperity and wealth. It is also believed to improve one's sense of humor.

Bloodstone - as its name suggests, Bloodstone is a good blood cleanser. It aids blood circulation and regulates blood flow. Therefore, it is recommended for patients suffering from leukemia. This gem detoxifies the spleen, kidneys, intestines, bladder, and liver. Bloodstone is good for people who are experiencing low energy and a weak immune system. Aside from improving energy by releasing blockages, it also improves stamina and endurance.

Jade – Ancient Chinese practitioners were the pioneers of using Jade as a healing stone. It is known as a cleansing stone. It promotes the good performance of the body's filtration systems and elimination organs. Jade balances the fluid ratio (such as the alkaline-acid ratio) in the body and removes toxins. It also helps in the healing of skeletal and cellular systems. Jade is recommended to patients who have just undergone reconstructive or plastic surgeries because of its abilities to ease pain. This gem is a good companion for goal-setting as it helps you fulfill your dreams into reality. It is a stone of abundance and prosperity.

Kambaba Jasper – this stone aids in the performance of the digestive system and boosts the immune system. It helps in cellular growth and provides soothing effects to the nerves. Kambaba Jasper helps ensure that minerals and vitamins are properly distributed in the body. It is also a gem of fertility. Kambaba Jasper brings alignment of the mind, body, and spirit. Being the stone of tranquility and peace, it relieves stress and gives you the courage to face your fears.

Malachite – this elegant-looking stone has the power to protect you from being sickly. It is recommended for women as it has healing abilities of feminine ailments. It promotes fertility and eases menstrual pain. Malachite clears and restores the heart chakra. It boosts mental clarity to release unfocused thoughts and chaotic feelings.

Moss Agate - Out with old, in with new; Moss Agate releases old habits and encourages fresh beginnings. It has strong vibrations from the earth and nature; making it a crystal for abundance and wealth. Moss Agate prevents swelling in the body by aiding the smooth flow of lymphatic system. It acts as anti-inflammatory to the body.

Ruby Zoisite – Ruby Zoisite has the ability to heal the emotions; especially of those suffering from depression. It is a blend of earthy Zoisite and feisty Ruby. Since it is the crystal for patience and passion, it can also heal the heart and align both female and male energies. Ruby Zoisite is said to heal ailments relating to gynecological issues like infertility.

<u>Orange Crystals</u>

Orange crystals are associated with the sacral chakra. Resembling the power of the sun, orange colors awaken the passion of the spirit. They have a trace of red's fiery characteristics, but are toned down with a lighter spirit. Orange crystals awaken the sense of creativity, confidence, and enthusiasm. Orange is a strong color that also reflects personal power. They add a little spice in life by strengthening creativity while helping you go with the flow, especially when undergoing a transitional phase in life. Orange crystals create a flicker in your inner fire to encourage you to be more creative and move forward in life.

Orange Calcite - a stone for sexuality and creativity, Orange Calcite is an energizing stone that promotes positive energy. It is recommended to bring an Orange Calcite with you whenever you are about to enter a new phase in life. This stone is recommended to those who are often bothered with suicidal thoughts, as it has protective energies from self-harm.

Tangerine Quartz – Tangerine Quartz is a stone of the sacral chakra. It encourages sexuality, creativity, and sexual balance. Therefore, it helps you maintain a good balance between your giving and receiving qualities in terms of relationships with others.

Pink Crystals

Being the shade of compassion and love, pink crystals are meant to heal the heart chakra. These are big-time openers of the heart. The color pink is a blend of red and white. Red represents the heart's fiery emotions, but is softened by the color white which is soothing and pure. Pink crystals help bring you into a life overflowing with compassion, acceptance, and comfort. Having a feminine color, pink crystals are also the stones for beauty. They have gentle and soft energies; promoting warmth to the heart and soul. They encourage discernment, creativity, and a deeper connection to your environment as well. Pink crystals also bring professional help as they release stress and negative thoughts. Physically, they help heal problems related to the body's blood sugar levels.

Kunzite - Kunzite is called The Mother's Stone because it is suitable for young mothers bothered by the challenges of raising kids. It especially helps put young children to sleep, and helps them have a good night rest as well. Kunzite is a powerful stone that can heal anxiety and depression. It can also help people who are battling with addiction. In terms of physical healing, it boosts the circulatory system and promotes stronger heart muscles.

Lemurian Quartz – the healing properties of a Lemurian Quartz are associated with the treatment of circulatory disorders and spinal problems. It promotes stronger vein structures and cleanses the body from harmful toxins. It is also beneficial for the healing of cellular memory and is recommended to those who have just suffered from a stroke. A crystal dubbed as a "stairway to heaven", Lemurian Quartz promotes oneness and encourages you to love your individuality.

Lithium Quartz - one of the most eye-catching gems, Lithium Quartz has a soft pink color brought about by its natural lithium component. Lithium is widely used in the making of anti-anxiety and antidepressant pills. Therefore, Lithium Quartz can help to heal mental illnesses. It has a blend of both strong and mild properties that promote physical, spiritual, and mental balance.

Rhodonite - known as the "Rescue Crystal", Rhodonite has strong healing properties that drive away the sense of fear. It is the gem for compassion and forgiveness; therefore, it aids in the healing of problematic relationships. If your relationship has brought you a lot of trauma and you feel that all your emotional and physical energy has been depleted because of it, then, Rhodonite is the stone for you. It can also help in the healing of stomach ulcers and liver diseases.

Rose quartz - Another well-known feminine stone, Rose Quartz heals the heart chakra and opens it up to attract all kinds of love - romantic love, self- love, love of country, love of everything in the universe. Since it is a strong crystal for the heart, it is good for healing emotional pain. It also boosts confidence or self-esteem. Rose quartz aids in the healing of ailments related to heart health, and promotes good blood circulation. It makes the heart muscles stronger; thus, helping to prevent heart attacks and thrombosis. It is also known to heal insomnia, depression, and other mental illnesses.

Grey Crystals

The color grey represents the vastness of the universe since it is a shade of the moonlight. Grey crystals are known as protective stones. They encourage retreat and rest. Therefore, grey crystals are helpful to those who are overwhelmed with their world.

Using a grey crystal can encourage you to take a little pause first in order to heal your unrecognized emotional wounds.

Hematite — Hematite has been a healing stone since ancient times because of its iron content. It can heal ailments related to the circulatory system; especially the heart. Since it is an earthy stone, it takes away negativities in the body; hence, making you calmer. It also helps you feel more centered and balanced; developing your sense of logical thinking.

Shungite - Around two billion years old in existence, Shungite is also known as the "Earth's Miracle Molecule" because it can absorb hazardous health energies in the body. It is also a powerful stone for the detoxification of the body.

<u>Purple Crystals</u>

Having an undeniable magical luster, purple crystals possess the power of amplifying energies. Being known as the color of intuition and enlightenment, purple provides a soothing effect and healing to the emotions, especially when used together with other heart chakra gems. Purple crystals radiate an exotic and passionate appeal. Purple crystals are symbols of royalty, magic, good judgement, and mystery. They provide soothing effects to the nerves; helping you release unwanted thoughts. They can lift your mood and bring back your emotions into total balance even just by holding them.

Amethyst – Amethyst has the properties to heal one's state of peace. It is a good stone for dealing with stress and anxiety. It is a stone that opens up more than simply the intuition, and encourages spiritual growth and inner strength. Amethyst is the best of both worlds - it can simultaneously attract positive energy while clearing the negative. Physically, Amethyst can heal ailments in the endocrine system and hormonal problems. It is a good stone for strengthening the immune system, and acts as an aide in metabolism. It has blood cleansing properties as well. Amethyst is recommended to patients who are recovering from cancer. It is good for treating headaches since it has a powerful combination of calming and healing effects.

Lepidolite - Lepidolite is naturally made of an element called Lithium, making it a perfect gem for relieving anxiety and stress. It encourages relaxation and brings emotional calmness. This stone is recommended especially for those who are going through a difficult and painful transition in their life; such as when mourning. Lepidolite can help them easily get over the phase of mourning and find reasons to feel happiness again.

Red Crystals

Red crystals are associated with the root chakra since red represents life force and passion. They have the power to energize the body, mind, and spirit. Red crystals also promote courage and motivation. If you need an extra lift in order to achieve a dream, or if you simply want to revive your lust for life, red crystals can bring back inspiration and passion into your life. They also symbolize prosperity, warmth, and vitality.

Garnet – this gem boosts the physical energy levels and strengthens the immune system. It regenerates DNA and purifies the blood, heart and lungs. This crystal suits the root chakra well as it keeps you grounded and aligned to yourself. It is a passion crystal that promotes good flow of energies all throughout the body. Garnet is also popular for its ability to attract both love and wealth into your life. It is also a stone for passion and inspiration; promoting strong and lasting relationships.

Red Jasper - a stone for motivation, Red Jasper heals low energy levels in the body; giving you more vitality to take action in life. This stone is recommended to those who actively exercise. It can speed up and enhance the effects of exercise since it has the ability to generate muscle tissue. It also encourages a positive attitude, stability, and protection. Red Jasper is also a feminine stone for self-confidence and empowerment.

Sunstone – Sunstone is used in healing stomach ulcers and a sore throat. This stone is recommended to those who always have nightmares. As its name suggests, Sunstone has a very strong connection to the energies of the sun. Therefore, it is a happy and light stone. It has protective properties and promotes strength, creativity, power, and leadership qualities.

White Crystals

These are good healing stones since white represents purification and transformation; symbolizing light after a period of darkness. White crystals have strong psychic energies as they are ruled by the moon. They work well together with any other crystal, or can even be used as substitute to any kind of color. White crystals help revive peace, serenity and calmness in your life. They are also feminine stones which represent birth and regeneration, freedom, and hope.

Apophyllite - Known as the stone that emanates light to recharge the soul, Apophyllite is good for the healing of one's inner problems of worry and fear. It is a highly vibrational stone that also fights anxiety and stress. When used in meditation, it can bring a very strong connection to the spiritual realm. Sometimes, people find Apophyllite very overwhelming because of its strong spiritual powers. When using this stone in meditation, make sure to prepare a bottle of water or a small amount of food to keep you grounded after the spiritual experience.

Clear Quartz – Clear Quartz is considered as a master healer and is applicable to almost any kind of physical or emotional condition. This crystal is commonly used as the base of healing layouts as it strengthens the energies of other crystals that it comes in contact with. It brings balance in the body by enhancing the energy flow and stimulating the circulatory and immune systems. It is said to heal ailments like vertigo, motion sickness or dizziness, and migraines. It also aids in metabolism and weight loss. As its name suggests, Clear Quartz promotes mental clarity and helps attract the fulfillment of all your other intentions.

Moonstone - this is one of the most feminine crystals. Known as the gem of destiny, it has strong vibrations from the moon which balances the feminine energies in the body. This is best for women who want to attract fertility. It also promotes the proper rhythm of the body's biological forces; aiding in the proper growth of children and slowing the degeneration of the elderly. It helps maintain healthy hair, skin, eyes and the fleshy organs of the body.

Selenite – In terms of physical healing, Selenite aids in the treatment of cancers and tumors. It helps in the healing of ailments related to the skeletal system. Healing and clearing the body from negative energies is an easy task for a Selenite. It is a stone for cleansing. It heals the mind by encouraging mental clarity and a calming sense of peace.

Rainbow Crystals

Blessed with the natural colors of life, rainbow crystals are good reminders to keep enjoying and appreciating the natural beauty that surrounds you. They represent hope, optimism, peace, happiness, and courage. Rainbows are scientifically known to be produced by light. Therefore, every rainbow crystal is a reminder that light cannot pass through someone's life if his/her mind and heart are closed. Rainbow crystals are natural emotional healers.

Flame Aura Quartz – in terms of physical healing, this gem aids in the treatment of bone diseases including Multiple Sclerosis. It also helps in the treatment of diabetes. It helps in stimulating the immune system of people diagnosed with AIDS. This gem is also known as rainbow quartz or titanium quartz. It lessens someone's sense of doubt and fear. Its rainbow energy helps awaken your sense of spiritual purpose.

Fluorite - Fluorite is the crystal for the mind; giving you a clear mental state and sharper focus. This gem is recommended for people who are suffering from learning disabilities and attention deficit disorder because it helps in battling distractions. It helps stop narrow-mindedness, and aids in attracting creativity and new ideas into your life. In terms of physical healing, Fluorite helps in the treatment of skin problems. It also heals ailments related to the respiratory system, brain, nerves, and even allergies and colds.

Conclusion

Once again, thanks for taking the time to read this book all about crystal healing.

At this stage, you should have a good understanding of the different crystals that can be used for healing, and how to use them for a variety of benefits!

Now it's time to gather your desired crystals, and begin using them to enhance your own life, and the lives of those around you.

Finally, if you enjoyed this book, please take the time to leave me a review on Amazon. The positive feedback really helps me to continue producing these books!